THE AGE TO COME

About the author

David Boyle has been writing about new ideas for more than a quarter of a century. He is a fellow of the New Economics Foundation and a former independent reviewer for the Cabinet Office. He is the author of *The Tyranny of Numbers*, *The Human Element*, *Blondel's Song* and *Authenticity: Brands, Fakes, Spin and the Lust for Real Life*. He lives in the South Downs.

The Age to Come

Authenticity, post-modernism and how
to survive what comes next

A collection of essays by David Boyle

THE REAL PRESS

www.therealpress.co.uk

Published in 2016 by the Real Press; first published by
Endeavour Press in 2013.

www.therealpress.co.uk © David Boyle

ISBN (print) 978-1530087785

Contents

Foreword

Everyone says we are in the 'post-modern' age. It is a prevailing philosophy that everything is relative and nothing is quite real – where we are overwhelmed by an explosion of meaningless 'signifiers' and ironic gobbledegook. Those are our times, and it is hard to imagine the post-modern age ending and a new cultural age emerging – dominating our arts, culture and beliefs.

But the signs are there. Something is happening deep below the culture. That is the subject of these essays, who date from the period after the publication of my book *Authenticity: Brands, Fakes, Spin and the Lust for Real Life*. Where that book led me was the strong sense that change was in the air and that the demand for authenticity was a bigger shift than I had realised. It was more than the latest whim of exhausted consumers; it was a trend that somehow crossed cultural boundaries.

It seemed to me to be a clue about where we were all going. Where that is exactly I am still not quite sure about, but these essays provide some clues. The main essay, *The Age to Come,* was written especially for this publication to draw together some of the strands and to provide a pointer to the future. I may not be right, but something is happening and I hope these essays, and the title essay in particular will start people talking a bit about how the world is changing and about the emerging age which will dominate our children's lives.

I would like to thank the original publishers of the essays here for permission to reprint them. They were originally published as:

'The most artificial place on earth No. 1: Ocean Dome', *The Ecologist*, Oct 2003.

In search of *wabi-sabi* planning: The strange revival of authentic places', *Town and Country Planning*, Dec 2004.

'Is there such a thing as a community brand?', *Viewpoint*, No 17, 2005.

'Everything today is thoroughly modern – or is it?', *Town and Country Planning*, May 2006.

'Authenticity' in L Bouckaert and L Zsolnai, *The Palgrave Handbook of Spirituality and Business*,

'The lunch, the cook and the larder', *Ethical Junction* (www.ethical-junction.org), Feb 2007.

David Boyle, February 2013

The Age to Come

*"Beauty is truth, **truth beauty**, – that is all*
Ye know on earth, and all ye need to know."
John Keats, 'Ode on a Grecian urn', 1819

We live in simultaneous ages, and sometimes they are only given names when we are dead and gone. It is peculiar that we should live in a country and never be told its name.

The Renaissance historians named the 'dark ages' and 'middle ages' that had gone before. Modern historians have their 'Victorian Age' or 'Age of the Enlightenment'. Most of us think more in terms of decades. But there are other ages and in some ways they are more meaningful, because they sum up the prevailing philosophies of life that dominate the moment in time that is ours.

The great cultural movements start with a flicker of interest in the *avant garde*, reacting against the prevailing abominations. Then they grow to dominate thinking in politics, the arts, literature, design, marketing and even economics and politics. Then they are in turn swept away by the next prevailing philosophy, and which answer people's need for direction, frameworks, attitude and much more.

For those of us with a short attention span, these great philosophical ages might come and go unnoticed every half a century or so, perhaps less. They are heralded and die, unremarked by the mass of humanity. But they are potent – and much more potent than you would think for the earnest and obscure debate about them among earnest and obscure academics.

I was born in 1958. It was the year of Sputnik and CND but it was also the time that modernism had finally emerged from the hothouse of German architecture salons, arts cafés, and intellectual magazines. Benjamin Britten and John Cage both had modernist works performed that year. The smooth and modern Time-Life Building and the Seagram Building, both in New York City, had their scaffolding and covers removed. A modernist typhoon was gathering around the urban form of the big cities. The Lloyd's of London building, and the historic Palace and Gaiety theatres, all bit the dust that year. Thousands of white or grey towers to house the poor were on the agenda in every housing authority. It was also the year that the fightback began: the Victorian Society was founded; the old fogies were arming the selves for a battle.

Throughout my childhood, the transformation of modernism from *avant garde* obscurity into a prevailing philosophy for urban living was emerging, and the sounds of battle were everywhere. There was Jane Jacobs and her fellow New York mothers challenging city planner Robert Moses and his plan for urban motorways. There was the poet John Betjeman, defending the doomed Euston Arch, and whose *Collected Poems* became a bestseller that year. The very word 'progress' seemed to have been co-opted by the modernist forces, in unstoppable alliance with the developers and highway planners.

But there came a point when the challenge became overwhelming, and the architectural critic Charles Jencks dated that moment very specifically: "Modern architecture died in St Louis, Missouri on July 15 1972 at 3.32 pm (or thereabouts)," he wrote. Jencks was the prophet of what he called 'post-modernism', but it was architecture he was particularly interested in. The date he chose for the end of one philosophical age and the start of another was the moment of the planned explosion that demolished the Pruitt-Igoe Flats in Chicago, one of the most egregious examples of modernism as prisons for the poor. But that was back in 1972. It was much clearer a decade after the destruction of Pruitt-Igue that some new approach was emerging.

I first grasped what post-modernism might be when I saw the strange pastiche of ancient Egyptian art that was the new Homebase store in Kensington around 1985. You could see the same underlying objectives in the pastiche buildings, like Robert Venturi's Chippendale-style skyscraper. The modernists regarded this as an outrageous betrayal of their values. More of that in a moment.

But here is the question. If post-modernism is the defining frame for our own age, then what is coming next? Can we see something emerging already? The answer, which this essay attempts to make, is that you can.

We are deep inside the post-modern age now. It is hard to imagine a style that is somehow different from the Art Deco pastiches, the Tudor pastiches, the classical pastiches going up in concrete everywhere we look. Or the novels about sad middle-aged men that take place simultaneously now and in 1848. Or the bizarre inability of the fine arts world to go beyond *épater les bourgeois,* when the bourgeois they wanted to shock have long since packed up and left the stage.

The fine arts world gives the game away. Modernism reached its zenith when the money began to follow it. It became no longer a brave critique of the status quo, but the status quo itself. The same thing has happened to post-modernism, now that the Brit Art revolution – with its irony and jokes – has become the establishment. It is no longer a brave critique of modernism, an ironic understanding of the social construction of reality, a response to the linguistic philosophies of Jacques Derrida and Michel Foucault. It is where the money is, riding the virtual wave, virtual reality and all the rest. It sits on the throne and dominates our lives. So the time cannot be too far away when it becomes a caricature of itself, and – with another great intellectual clash – dissolves into history, leaving behind the seeds of the next age.

What comes next will dominate our children's lives, and maybe our grandchildren's lives as well, before it eventually compromises with the prevailing economic orthodoxy as well, and is swept away in its turn.

The next age, the coming age, will try to challenge our contemporary conviction that nothing is true and everything is relative. It will not reach back hopelessly to previous ages of certainty, though people may accuse it of that: we have lost our innocence about social reality. It will not pretend it is somehow possible to work out unambiguously what is true in this world. It will not turn its back on the understanding and tolerance we have generated with the social construction of knowledge. But it will not be limited by that any more.

We are moving into an age that will try to satisfy our need for what we have lost, looking around for something we *can* be sure of – something we can use to measure everything else against – and it is beginning to find it in ourselves and our humanity, and will use that to seek a way out of the paralysis of post-modernism.

How do I know? Because although the new age is not yet upon us, the critique of post-modernism is beginning to emerge that will bring a new project – and these great ages are, each of them, a project to find directions out of the dead ends thrown up by the project before. We can't know for sure the parameters of the coming age – the new age of humanism – but we can begin to glimpse a few features. And, as they say, forewarned is forearmed...

"Our culture expects us to be manic – to over produce, to over consume, and to waste – but in all this, something vital is missing: the knowledge that life can be transformed by a sacramental experience."
Suzi Gablik, *Has Modernism Failed?*, 1984

Post-modernism died in Washington, DC, on Monday 21 January 2013, at 5.54pm (or thereabouts). Not because that was the moment that Beyoncé mimed 'The Star-Spangled Banner' at Barack Obama's second inauguration as president, but because the fact that she did not actually perform live was the main point of discussion around the world. Brooklyn band Prince Rama said: "I actually think Beyoncé lip-syncing the national anthem is one of the best conceptual art pieces I've seen in a long time". There was the clue – was it such a matter of comment because post-modern values have not yet run their course, or because authenticity actually matters to people?

Well, I am copying Charles Jencks' style. It would also be appropriate for the death of post-modernism to be marked by a deeply insignificant event which caused headlines around the virtual world. Post-modernism is the age where people "rise without trace", as Christopher Booker once said of David Frost. The point about Beyoncé's lip-syncing is that all the tenets of post-modernism suggest it should not be important at all. What is 'real' after all? What is Beyoncé beyond a culturally conditioned artifact, a *signifier* who is mediated through a whole series of different media languages, manipulated by a whole range of computer-generated amplifications of style and substance?

The complaint that Beyoncé's performance at the inauguration was not completely real makes no sense in a post-modern world. The fact that people *did* complain implies that they think something else is important, and because it grated alongside the commitment to honesty and transparency in Obama's inauguration speech just before.

The question is: is this an example of people clinging to authenticity long after such an idea was banished to the realms of the hopelessly conservative – or is it a sign that, actually, all is not right in the post-modern condition? That is my contention here – and not just about Beyoncé either, but the increasing demand that people are expressing for something real, un-manipulated, un-marketed, un-mediated, direct and human.

I am arguing that this is an important shift, and that it represents not just dogged human awkwardness – an opposition to the way the powerful forces of the world are ranged behind the post-modern worldview that all is relative, backed by the combined chequebooks of the corporate world. It represents a new longing to seek out what remains authentic which will propel us into a new project – to find what binds us together as human beings, to find the authentic kernel of reality, and to defend it.

But to understand why I am arguing this, we need to travel back to the first glimmerings of the modernist revolt which emerged from the years before the First World War.

We can see the remains of the previous 'modern' age all around us, in those glass towers, those white neat lines, that fanatical obsession with honesty – that form should follow function. The fascination with efficiency and with factories, and the idea that houses were, as the architect Le Corbusier put it, "machines for living in". For the modernists gathering round the new Bauhaus School under Walter Gropius in 1919, pretence, bluff and ornamentation were deceits which had led to the horrors of the trenches.

Modernism was an elite project and deliberately so. The critic Suzi Gablik explained that, "between 1910 and 1930, art cut itself loose from its social moorings and withdrew, to save its creative essence". By 1961, there were only an estimated 25 modern artists working in New York City. All that was to change over the following decade, but this withdrawal was part of modernism's declaration of independence. "Art no longer cares to serve the state and religion," said Kasimir Malevich.

For the post-modernists, in the age that was to come, this was just meaningless – just as Malevich's black square, which he saw as a carrier of spiritual value, was just a culturally conditioned facade, without depth.

The challenge to the modernists began to emerge in the 1970s. The art critic of the London *Evening Standard*, Richard Cork, argued that modernists had become decadent and elitist under capitalism. His exhibition at the Serpentine Gallery in 1978, called 'Art for Whom?', sharpened the British end of the British revolt. On the other side of the Atlantic, Jencks traced the term 'post-modern' back to the 1930s, when it was used as an insult – these terms often begin their lives as insults. There was Jane Jacobs gaining the upper hand in New York City with her campaign for bustle in the streets. There was the Italian novelist Umberto Eco sketching out plans for a new kind of novel, brought to brilliant fruition in *The Name of the Rose*, using traditional language and shapes in new ironic ways. There were the ideas of the French literary critics filtering down through the universities. If modernism began with artists and found expression in art critics like Roger Fry, post-modernism began with writers and found expression in the works of literary critics.

All philosophical ages have an obsession with truth. For the modernists it lay in the pure, unembellished line. For the post-modernists, it was lost in a blooming, buzzing confusion of signs and cultural signifiers, beyond recovery. It was a rococo response to a Puritanism that had begun to lose its purpose. "I define post-modernism as incredulity towards meta-narratives," wrote the philosopher Jean-Francois Lyotard in his 1979 book *The Post-Modern Condition*. It was hardly surprising that the old guard was cross.

And they were. In October 1981, the French newspaper *Le Monde* published an article under the headline 'Décandence' which borrowed Marx's phrase that "a spectre is haunting Europe". In this case, the spectre was called 'post-modernism'.

That same year, the Dutch modernist architect Aldo van Eyck gave a lecture called 'Rats, Posts and Other Pests', which ended with this call to arms: "Ladies and gentlemen, I beg you: hound them down and let the foxes go!"

Again that same year, the modernist Berthold Lubetkin compared post-modernists to Hitler and Stalin. Many modernists regarded the kitsch, populist elements of the new age as reminiscent of Fascism and assumed it was just as repressive. Nothing could have been further from the truth. It was fun.

Looking back, it was the emergence of Andy Warhol among the handful of elite modernist artists in New York, with his fascination for irony, mass reproduction and mass culture, who had first struggled to express the new age (he had eight cats, all called 'Sam'). But it was already there, on the streets, in the Summer of Love and the revolt against the puritanical neatness of modernism.

It is now getting on for half a century since then, and it has become clear that post-modernism has its limitations too. The great engine of post-modern diversity, the internet, has been parcelled up among the great corporations. A hunger for something beyond the extremes of relativism is becoming clear, which knows that authenticity must be culturally conditioned – but searches for it anyway. Which refuses to acknowledge that men, women, people of different races or different classes, really can't understand or communicate with each other at all.

If modernism was a deeply-held belief in the perfectability of mankind by honest lines, post-modernism rejected belief of any kind. If modernism was an elitist project turned in on itself, post-modernism rejected elitism in all its forms. "For the committed modernist, the audience doesn't exist," wrote Suzi Gablik; you might add that, for the committed post-modernist, the *artist* doesn't exist.

I suppose I have made the same kind of journey as everyone else. Two decades ago, when I was writing a book about the future of cities, I was more than happy to embrace post-modern pastiche. It was fun, after all. It was everything those po-faced, puritanical modernists were not – with their brutal concrete structures they expected everyone else to live in. If the truth was so awful that it led to buildings like that, then let's bury it, I thought. "Less is a bore," said the post-modern architect Robert Venturi, paraphrasing Mies van der Rohe's dictum 'less is more', and I absolutely agreed.

I now see it rather differently. I can see the attractions in not believing in anything, in clinging to no truths, in giving up the struggle to know anything for certain. It is tolerance of a kind. But equally, it provides no signposts to the future, and no hope. Nor am I alone in that frustration with the post-modern status quo, and most of all the frustration with the post-modern scepticism about humanity – the attempt to define humanity in such a way that no distinction is possible any more between real and virtual. Because human beings *are* just glorified computers (so they say).

Francis Fukuyama, the influential author of *The End of History*, was even able to talk about "abolishing human beings as such" within a couple of generations, so that "a new post-human history will begin". MIT's Marvin Minsky talked about the advent of "artificial scientists, artists, composers and personal companions". Even the head of BT's laboratory Peter Cochrane looked forward to a "creeping evolution towards a cyborg world of partially artificial people".

"So what separates us and our noisy neurons from those in the latest machines?" he asked in 1999. "Only scale and sensors. Our awareness comes from sight, sound, touch, smell and taste. We can now give all of this to a machine in a form that could be superior to ours."

In the end, post-modernism provides no defence of what it means to be human, which is the source of the new authenticity which the age to come will seek. The post-modern advocate of artificial intelligence Ray Kurzweil suggests that the first artificial brain will be developed by 2029. The simplest computer has long since exceeded the memory and calculating skills of the cleverest human being. The computer Deep Blue beat the chess champion Gary Kasparov in 1995, it was a formative moment for the age that is to come. Because the challenge is now to set out what it is that human beings can do which no machine ever can – they can create, they can love and they can care.

But it builds on a scientific insight, emerging out of the ripples from the science of chaos. Thanks to people like the theoretical physicist David Bohm and others, we know that the whole is more than the sum of its parts. Thanks to what we know about the new study of collective intelligence, we know that the whole can be wiser than the parts. We know there is more to truth than the bits and pieces that make it up, just as there is more to a human being than the chemicals and energy they can be separated into. These are controversial ideas – of course they are: we are still knee-deep in post-modernism – but they are the seeds from which the age to come will grow.

If modernism was a reaction against the lies and half-truths of the First World War, and a project to find truth, post-modernism was a reaction against neatness, industrial systems and assembly line thinking. The new humanist age will be a reaction against the hollowness of the post-modern world, the reductionism of our one-dimensional systems and shiny, one-dimensional culture. It will be a reaction against the virtual mesh without individual authors or creativity, where real and unreal blur together – where individuals are hopelessly isolated in mutual misunderstanding and cultural barriers.

As the American philosopher Robert Nozick put it: "In a virtual world, people will long for reality even more." That search for reality, and the depth that lies behind it, is the grand project of the age that is to come.

*

"A market atmosphere with its constant demands for something new, is highly unfavourable to the creation of authentic and permanent values."
Suzi Gablik, *Has Modernism Failed?*, 1984

When the eminently post-modern artist Tracey Emin told her then boyfriend, the poet Billy Childish, that he was "stuck, stuck, stuck!" – neither of them realised that it would provide the name to an art movement. The Stuckists began with eleven members in 1999, and now has groups in 52 different countries, covering writers, photographers and musicians.

The Stuckists began as a revolt against the establishment's single-minded obsession with the more vacuous conceptual art, which had its roots in Marcel Dechamp's famous urinal exhibited in New York in 1917, but has progressed so little further since. More recently, they have declared that their objective is to re-discover modernism, so they may not thank me for dragging them into my own assertions about the future. Whether or not Stuckism *sticks* remains to be seen, but the original manifesto drafted by Billy Childish and Charles Thomson in 1999 has all the hallmarks of the coming age. "Stuckism is the quest for authenticity," they wrote:

"By removing the mask of cleverness and admitting where we are, the Stuckist allows him/herself uncensored expression. Painting is the medium of self-discovery. It engages the person fully with a process of action, emotion, thought and vision, revealing all of these with intimate and unforgiving breadth and detail. Stuckism proposes a model of art which is holistic. It is a meeting of the conscious and unconscious, thought and emotion, spiritual and material, private and public."

Here are many of the themes of the age to come set out clearly: the project to bring together these atomised elements of the human experience, healing the breach between the spiritual and material – and, above all, re-discovering human skills. "Artists who don't paint aren't artists," said the Stuckist manifesto. This was partly a challenge to the art schools which had made their drawing and painting teachers redundant, but it also reflects similar themes in the new age – the 'Great Reskilling' of the Transition Towns movement, the crafts movement, resurgent at Etsy.com

"Post-modernism, in its adolescent attempt to ape the clever and witty in modern art, has shown itself to be lost in a cul-de-sac of idiocy. What was once a searching and provocative process (as Dadaism) has given way to trite cleverness for commercial exploitation," said the manifesto. "The Stuckist calls for an art that is alive with all aspects of human experience; dares to communicate its ideas in primeval pigment; and possibly experiences itself as not at all clever... If it is the conceptualist's wish to always be clever, then it is the Stuckist's duty to always be wrong."

The year 1999 was an important moment of revolt against the post-modern order. It was the year of the Post-Autistic Economics revolt by economics students at the Sorbonne, accusing their teachers of ignoring the real world and obsession with figures, theorems and abstractions. It seemed to mesh in with the Dogme (1995) film-makers in Denmark, and the 'New Puritan' writers in the UK (2001), who were struggling to express some kind of authenticity in their new medium. The Stuckists' 'Remodernism' manifesto was translated into a Remodernist manifesto for film-making by the artist Jesse Richards in 2008, which – though it looked back to modernism – actually played with ideas around spirituality and *wabi-sabi*, that I regard as part of the coming age.

This is the new humanist project: to find

beauty, wholeness, truth, humanity, authenticity, depth. To go beneath the surface, to suck what is left of ultimate meaning through pieces of straw, to knit together the diverse and atomised strands of human culture into something whole, real and distinctively human – set free by the rejection of post-modernism to learn from...

... nature. At last we can look at Antoni Gaudi's unfinished masterpiece, the extraordinary creation that is Barcelona Cathedral, La Sagrada Familia, and begin to understand the sinewy, organic walls, arising out of the earth as if this building was alive. This is the essence of the coming age – learning from natural structures in architecture, from natural patterns in economics and the other social sciences, from natural methods of survival, to create beauty. The challenge from a changing climate requires us not so much to confront nature, but to learn from it to survive. The colourful, organic exuberance of the Hundertwasser House in Vienna – with its waving lines and bright colours and bizarre balconies – so uncategorisable before, is a pioneering sign of what is to come, designed by a prophet of the coming age.

... the past. Historian David Edgerton's 2006 book *The Shock of the Old* described how, despite the rhetoric of rapid technological change, the reverse is also true – I have been travelling in Boeing 747s my entire life, after all. The new age is indicated by organisations like Slow Food, Slow Money and Slow Education, which all look back to the past for inspiration, but try to adapt it for the future. This is not conservatism; it is the ability to learn from the past but to use it to knit it together with modern knowledge to create solutions.

... artists. Before the First World War, it was taken for granted that artists were involved in the future of society and the debate about its future direction. The modernists altered that dynamic, turning away from public debate, suspicious of political rhetoric – but asserting an efficient vision of a shiny technological future even so. The post-modernists found asserting the future a meaningless activity – whose future, they asked? The coming age will re-assert the position of the artist, and one of the pioneers is the virtual reality pioneer Jaron Lanier, whose book *You Are Not a Gadget* describes the development of what he calls digital Maoism, where artists become a new proletariat toiling for the benefit of an all-powerful virtual bourgeoisie. Lanier's target has been the idea that individual creativity should be undermined by the internet, because the post-modern prophets of a digital future are toiling towards a day when there will be no individual books, pictures or musical compositions; just one 'mashed' whole.

... systems thinkers. Modernism in practice was a limiting system, a stultifying bureaucracy masquerading as efficiency. Post-modernism has failed to break this pattern, because irony turned out not to be enough. The coming age will try to solve the problem by going local, because that is both human-scale and the place where all the strands genuinely come together in a complete system. It rejects one-dimensional measures of reality, communication that isolates people, hidden in-crowd moralities and the ethics of power without relationships. Already the strongest banks in the USA are the ones with local roots. There is a renaissance of local manufacturing just beginning because of high energy costs which undermine the economics of long-distance transport. In a recent *Fortune* article, the journalist Joshua Cooper Ramo wrote about the emerging consensus about the importance of joined-up cultures and ethics. "We've found that the firms that function best do so because of values and cultures," he wrote. "Megabrands are suffering a collapse in legitimacy, as we found what looks good outside ... is often weak on the inside." Depth again.

... spirituality. The modernists rejected conventional religion because it was, well, old-fashioned. The post-modernists rejected it because there seemed no way to choose one religion over another. It was meaningless to them. But the coming age will take another look at spirituality, because it is a consistent feature of being human and because it has depth. The coming age is a response to reductionism, and the idea – as Richard Dawkins put it – that we are no more than "bytes and bytes and bytes of digital information".

The grand project of the coming age is to learn from this and knit it together, to provide a definitive truth in an age that has come to believe there is no such thing, to celebrate humanity in an age which has come to believe it can be reduced to cultural conditioning and information systems, and to rediscover depth in an age which is sceptical of anything which lacks a shiny surface.

"It is the Stuckist's duty to always be wrong," said the Stuckist manifesto. As we go into the coming age, that is what it will feel like to be at the cutting edge.

The ages at a glance

	Modernist	Post-modernist	New Humanist
Emerging nation	Germany	France	UK
Presiding ethic	Truth	Tolerance	Wholeness
Besetting sin	Tidiness	Relativism	Obscurity
Inspiring technology	Assembly line	Internet	Solar cell
Primary language	Architecture	Literature	Narrative
Presiding genius	Walter Gropius	Jacques Derrida	David Bohm
Cheerleader	Roger Fry	Charles Jencks	*Position vacant*

*

"If you meet anything that's going to be human and isn't yet, or used to be human once and isn't now, or ought to be human and isn't, keep your eyes on it and feel for your hatchet."
C. S. Lewis, *The Lion, the Witch and the Wardrobe*, 1950

The final section of this essay tries to give a bit of advice to the outriders of the coming age and those who want to be. Here is a ten-point programme to hasten the new humanism:

1. Seek out products, people and possibilities which you feel are authentic.

2. Shun one-dimensional experiences, 'rationalised' one-dimensional systems, robots, computerised check-outs, fast food and – wherever possible – call centres with scripts.

3. End those qualms about finding the appropriate language for the target audience – it is all being swept away. Inspire them as human beings.

4. Have nothing in your house that you do not know to be useful, or believe to be beautiful

(William Morris, a post-modern cultural reference, I admit).

5. Build local institutions, face to face, and at human scale.

6. Ask the Little Boy's question in the Emperor's New Clothes as noisily as possible, whenever confronted with one-dimensional statistical 'truth' – yes, the school is high in the league tables, but is the education any good?

7. Meditate every day – or some other form of spiritual practice.

8. Be creative yourself once at least every 24 hours.

9. Grow a little of your own food.

10. Be wrong at every possible opportunity.

Is this the most artificial place on earth?

This article first appeared in *The Ecologist* in October 2003, shortly after the publication of my book *Authenticity*. It was intended to introduce readers to some of the ideas in the book, and described a visit I made to the strange inland artificial seaside resort in Japan, known as Ocean Dome.

It is real water, but that's about all that is genuine. Yet people who bathe in the artificial beach at Ocean Dome in Japan - with its artificial sunshine, artificial waves and artificial sand - expect something better than merely real. And therein lies the problem.

It is now nearly two decades since the novelist Umberto Eco wandered around California looking at 3-D versions of Leonardo da Vinci's painting of the Last Supper, describing the whole experience in an essay called 'Travels in Hyper-reality'. He coined the word to describe the constant assurances he was receiving that the Last Supper experience was the most moving moment of his life, and better than seeing the real thing.

Since then, we have been overwhelmed with the hyper-real, by fake tastes, fake breasts, fake sounds, fake food and fake places - all hyped by powerful marketing as if they were somehow 'better than real', but actually downright artificial.

The country that really does hyper-real is Japan, and the artificial beach known as Ocean Dome (motto: 'Paradise within a paradise') - with its sliding roof, its wave machine and its constant 30 degrees - is its most extreme expression. And since I was writing a book about authenticity, I felt I just had to see it myself.

Ocean Dome is part of the so-called Seagaia resort along the coastal highway outside the city of Myazaki in the far south of Japan. It is a longish journey from Tokyo, by train, plane and bus, before I drew up in the almost deserted forecourt. It was Friday afternoon, and my arrival at the ticket counter created a small stir. Either it's the well-known Japanese recession or hyper-real is not currently in vogue, but I appeared to be almost the only visitor. So I rented a pair of swimming trunks (orange with sailing ships on), and then it was a short semi-naked walk through the empty foyer and onto the beach itself.

The heat and humidity was inviting at first - like an overheated municipal swimming pool - but the size of the place was a shock. Ocean Dome is bigger than many ocean liners - over 1,000 feet long - and has space for 13,500 tons of salt water and 10,000 people, without the mild inconvenience of real salt water, real crabs, real seaweed or fish. But there were two less inviting aspects that quickly became apparent. One was the feel of the artificial beach under my toes, made from small white pebbles like those you find on graves in English churchyards. The other was the slight gloom. It was a beautiful summer's day outside, but the great dome above the beach stayed resolutely shut, for fear that the real world would tempt us away.

I watched an elderly lady paddling by herself and a couple of youngsters dashing in and out of the precisely regulated waves, and tried to pinpoint exactly why it was disconcerting. It was pleasantly warm, but it felt faintly like a gymnasium – and they always remind me of exams. Also, the palm trees were too perfect to be real. The fruit behind the counter turned out to be plastic, and the backdrop was painted with small clouds and a deep blue sky as the Pacific view outside probably should have been.

There was the sound of a waterfall up one end, and the piped sound of Swing Low Sweet Chariot – which you wouldn't, let's face it, get on a real beach. Up the other was a fake volcano, complete with various water slides, called Bali Ha'i. I wondered if it ever occurred to James Michener or Oscar Hammerstein, writing *Tales of the South Pacific* just after VJ Day, that their imaginary island would one day make it into a Japanese theme park.

There was something fascinating about Ocean Dome, but something unnerving too. I suppose the fear is that in the back of the mind is that this may soon be the only kind of beaches we've got left – having abandoned the rest into oil jetties or abandoned the rest to chemical jetties or oil slicks. And I realised that this is exactly what we have been told throughout my life – either by those who were excited about this brave new artificial future or by those who felt powerless to stop it. We have lived through more than half a century constantly being told that the future of food was artificial, the future of books, newspapers, medicine and schools was virtual. And that we would soon deal entirely with computerised teachers and doctors through online.

For most of that time, the predictions seemed only too true. Highly-paid technologists and corporate apologists told us that somehow anyone who sketched out a different kind of vision of the future were 'standing in the way of progress'. But if you look around today, despite Ocean Dome, McDonald's and Microsoft, the real world has been fighting back. Many of the technologies predicted over the past half century have come true, of course, but they haven't sent reality packing as we were led to expect.

We haven't had the genius machines, able to think for themselves (predicted in 1970). Or human embryo packets in shops (1966). Or robots to look after the elderly (1983). Or dish-making machines in the kitchen (1967). Or artificial moons instead of street-lighting (1968). Despite the millions being pumped into the idea of replacing biological human life with a mixture of genetic engineering, cryogenics, artificial intelligence and nano-technology, a powerful minority of the population seems determined to defend the human option.

In fact, everywhere we look, there is an unremarked struggle between real and artificial.

There is a quiet 'authentic' lobby, increasingly committed to real food, real culture, real politics, real schools, real community, real medicine, real culture, real stories...

They may eat fast food sometimes. They may shop online, but they also increasingly defend their right to an authentic option with increasing passion: GM genes, once released, threaten to turn the whole of agriculture fake.

They are the force behind the rise of local brands, real ale, reading groups, organic vegetables, slow food, poetry recitals, unmixed music, materiality in art and unbranded vintage fashions: all symptoms of the same thing – a demand for human-scale, face-to-face institutions and real experience. Perhaps that was the problem with Ocean Dome: there comes a point when people react against the fake.

Japanese theme parks have risen and fallen over the past decade. There was a reproduction of Hans Andersen's house in Hokkaido, robots of American movie stars at Tochigi-ken, a whole British-style village at Shizuoka and a reproduction of the *Santa Maria* in Osaka - which is bizarrely twice the size of the original (better than real?). Presumably they were afraid that the smallness of the ship that discovered America would disappoint tourists.

Japan's recession has done for many of them, and one Friday afternoon at Ocean Dome was enough to confirm rumours of its financial struggle. Since my visit, the whole Seagaia resort has been snapped up by the New York-based corporate raider Timothy Collins of Ripplewood Holdings – who has been buying up struggling Japanese businesses without being able to speak much Japanese. I wish him well with it – personally I could do without it, even after a demonstration of their wave machine that could produce ten-foot high waves for surfing at the press of a button, each one precisely the same as the last.

So after an hour or so writing postcards on the beach, I gave up. The real sunshine filtering through the glass at either end of the monstrous auditorium was just too tempting. And, after all, the real rolling waves of the Pacific were just a few hundred yards away on the other side of the highway.

In the head to head battle between real and unreal, I know which side I'm on.

In search of *wabi-sabi* planning

This article arose out of the huge success of the New Economics Foundation's 'clone town' campaign in 2004, and it attempted to look in a little more detail at what made town centres feel real. It also borrowed from the Japanese concept of 'wabi-sabi' which, at the time, I felt was key to the new idea of authenticity. The article appeared in *Town & Country Planning* in December 2004.

I was involved over the summer with the launch of a campaign by the New Economics Foundation called Clone Town Britain. Unlike some of the campaigns I have been involved with over the last couple of decades – when the result has often been less than thrilling – I was absolutely staggered by the response.

It is true that Clone Town Britain – an attempt to highlight the way that everywhere from Ashford to Aberdeen now looks almost exactly the same –

was sprung on the world during the so-called 'silly season', when the media is notoriously short of copy. But even so, not only was it covered by every national newspaper – with full- or double-page articles – but BBC radio's flagship *Today* programme devoted their entire Saturday edition to the subject, broadcast from an unsuspecting Boston in Lincolnshire.

The reaction was immediate. Local newspapers called to express their amazement at their own 'clone town' survey results – in the case of Reading, because it appeared to be what they called a "near perfect clone". Local campaigners called up to ask for advice. In one case, they said they had discovered their local regeneration area was to be barred to locally-owned shops, on the grounds that these would be 'untidy'. Even officials from regional development agencies called up, terrified that their favoured development areas might be described by anybody as 'cloned'. The whole event, still going strong – ahead of the publication of a final report in the spring – struck me as a real watershed.

People have had a deep-seated fear of this spread of identikit places for some time – even Pete Seeger's song about 'Little boxes made of ticky-tacky' expressed some of it even in the 1960s

– but until now the professionals dismissed such timidity as backward.

Worries of this kind have been rejected for the past couple of generations as a fear of progress, or simply a fear of change – which was all the 'progress' word came to mean.

Now the argument is not so clear. As a society, we no longer quite believe in progress – at least not that kind of progress without benefit or value, and are unconvinced of its inevitability. And just in terms of townscapes, we can see all around us all too clearly where this kind of narrow 'progress' ends. Bustling high streets, full of life become 'rationalised'. The shopkeepers who used to recycle what they earned between them, and create local wealth by so doing, re-organised into the ordered, mildly slavish employees of a retail combine.

Streets which a generation ago were full of life, light and individuality – and individuality, because it is the basis of specialisation, is a basic pre-requisite of regeneration – have become blank concrete walls with the occasional entrance to underground car parks. Or if you are lucky, a large air conditioning vent.

We have all seen similar. But for sceptics, I encourage people to walk down Lambeth High

Street, once home to the bustling local shops that supplied the households of William Blake and Captain Bligh – the haven of human activity that gave us the 'Lambeth Walk' and much else besides – now just rationalised concrete walls and a few air vents. It is not really human – this is landscape for cars, neat landscapes of the bureaucratic mind – and it is therefore not quite real. It certainly isn't 'progress'.

Probably the loss of human contact is the most serious disappearance from both the new clone towns and ghost towns that are emerging around the UK. That has serious repercussions for other aspects of life.

"One ordinary morning last winter, Bernie Jaffe and his wife Ann supervised the small children crossing at the corner," wrote Jane Jacobs, who – despite her hostility to Ebenezer Howard and English planners in general – is probably closer to the tradition of human-scale planning than anyone else alive. "[They] lent an umbrella to one customer and a dollar to another; took custody of two keys; took in some packages for people in the next building who were away; lectured two youngsters who asked for cigarettes; gave street directions; took custody of a watch to give the repair man across the street when he opened later..." and so on. She was describing two small owner-shopkeepers in a human place, and it is real in a way that the modern Lambeth High Street is simply not.

There is a parallel here between the emerging physical landscape and the emerging mental one. Jerry Mander, the American social critic, has argued for decades that there is an intimate connection between the landscape and what we see on television. The result is what he describes as "a homogenised mental landscape that nicely matches the franchises, freeways suburbs, high-rise buildings, clearcut and speeded-up physical life of the external universe."

In fact, his 1973 book *Four Arguments for the Elimination of Television* was originally called *The Freewayification of the Mind*. You can see what he means. Turn on the television and we get bland identikit programmes, interspersed with rather too many advertisements, and much the same when we leave the front door. We get reality TV-style architecture and planning: places that pretend to be real but actually are just fake environments where the producers are in control, and busily pulling the strings. Like *Big Brother* also, there are cameras everywhere. Like *Changing Places*, we get a few designers with inflated opinions of themselves dashing into people's homes, but the result is tacky and completely unliveable.

We get new buildings commissioned by corporations and designed by architects who have seem to have no interest in their impact at ground level or on the lives of ordinary people, who have to walk along the road underneath – out of sight of the 'brave' glass towers on the skyline – with an unremitting diet for the eyes of concrete or reflective glass.

"The trouble is that some people really seem to think that tall buildings are the devil's work," my cousin told me recently: he is an architect of tall buildings, egged on currently by London's mayor (Ken Livingstone). I don't know about the devil, but anything that makes the majority of people feel belittled, out of scale, and feeds them a steady street-level cornucopia of *faux* marble and air conditioning, seems to me to degrade their humanity.

We need to rediscover the skills of creating real places – real because they are human-scale and recognise that people have three-dimensions to their lives. Because they do not assume we are the single-dimensional machines that 'modern' rationalised, McDonaldised systems require.

People may not be able to define an 'authentic' place, but they can recognise one immediately. A friend of mine told a dinner party recently that he had bought a flat in Paris because the shops are 'real' there – and we all knew immediately what he meant. They are more likely to be owned by the person serving you. They sell fresh food made on the premises. They smell real, you can exchange the time of day in them. They are not the kind of shops that G. K. Chesterton dismissed as "branches of the accounting profession".

That makes up the kind of untidy landscape described by Jane Jacobs in 1960s New York real, and it makes the 'clone towns' so beloved of regeneration executives insidiously fake. People's rising concern about this issue, then, is a symptom of a rising awareness of this indefinable sense of authenticity in so many areas of life.

Take food, for example. Thirty years ago, we were told on *Tomorrow's World* that the vacuum-packed just-add-water beef stew eaten by the Apollo astronauts was the future of food, and hat kitchens would disappear altogether. But, although we do buy ready meals in their plastic-packaged millions, the culture is actually going another way entirely. Organic food is enjoying an explosion of interest on both sides of the Atlantic.

Cookery TV programmes and cookery books are some of the most popular. Farmers markets, stuffed with fresh produce straight from the farm, are popping up in towns and cities all over the country. The Campaign for Real Ale has transformed our drinking habits. This is not to say that the market for fast food has disappeared, but there is a growing demand for what is authentic, local and trustworthy.

This trend is true of many other areas of life. Despite all we have been told for the past 40 years by corporate technologists and globalisers – that the future is entirely global and virtual – there is a sizeable minority who are increasingly committed to real food, real culture, real politics, real schools, real community, real medicine, real culture, real stories... The rise of local brands, real ale, reading groups, organic vegetables, complementary medicine, slow food, poetry recitals, unmixed music, materiality in art and unbranded vintage fashions, are all symptoms of the same thing – a demand for human-scale, face-to-face institutions and real experience.

Advertisers have grasped the word 'real'. Marketeers are experimenting with products with a sense of authenticity about them. That is why the demand that places should be 'real' has been making itself heard. Real places are people places. Not the kind of 'festival marketplaces' that have overtaken the USA over the past generation. Nor the café culture inspired by Barcelona and so beloved of Richard Rogers, though both have their role.

Both these examples of 'fake real' assume that humanity is one-dimensional – that people are at the height of their human potential when they shop, or when they sit in coffee bars. They may occasionally enjoy doing either, but neither is the case. Places will not be real until we spread that sense of authenticity to the whole city – where people live as well as where they play. That is a challenge among the miserable tower blocks around Barcelona just as it is in the cloned high streets and blank walls of Britain.

So, to draw some threads together, there is an architectural element to authenticity – the sense of life in the places where people live and work – just as there is an economic element to it. Planning can potentially bring those two elements together. But how do we start creating real places now? Well, three rather futuristic suggestions:

- Start using Section 106 agreements in retailing to insist on a percentage of locally-owned shops.

- Extend the concept of monopoly to local or regional economies: one retailer might not have a monopoly across the UK, but it certainly might in a city region – and this is clearly anti-competitive.

- If it was possible to decide the rateable value of a development according to the number of blank concrete walls at street level – a clear cost in terms of local economic health and well-being – we might see more exciting offerings beginning to appear on the drawing board.

The heart of the matter is that the purpose of planning is the creation of places, and the profession has allowed itself to become involved in creating places that increasingly people feel are fake. It has involved itself in cookie-cutter regeneration schemes, with cloned retail nightmares that might as well be downtown Dallas. It has allowed itself to be drawn into the creaking and sheltered visions of big name architects who believe that combinations of city centre cafés and forests of phallic glass stumps are the key to the future. It has clung to the myths of modernism for too long, scared of what is old and human-scale. In short, it needs a sense of what the Japanese call *wabi-sabi*, the cult of the worn, comfortable and human.

Wabi means the beauty of simple things. *Sabi* is the charm of things that are frayed by their use over time. The combination comes very close to a meaningful definition of authenticity as understood by those who are starting to use the term. It means natural, human and decaying. It means the power of overlooked details. Wabi-sabi does not mean shabby or run-down: it means the authenticity of planning by accretion, of renewal piece by piece, of atmosphere from different dimensions of activity – the kind of regeneration that can retain people, history and tradition.

Wabi-sabi planning is the key to making places real. The users of places, not the tidy-minded who know what's best for them, are impatient for it.

Is there such a thing as a community brand?

This article first appeared in *Viewpoint* magazine in 2005, then the organ of the Future Laboratory in London. It tried to make sense of the way that the corporate world was beginning to wrestle with authenticity, and the difficulties they were having with it. I encountered the Nikeplatz stunt in Vienna at the end of 2003.

A two-storey glass exhibition centre appeared in one of Vienna's most famous junctions just over a year ago, announcing that one of the world's megabrands had decided to rename the whole square. Karlsplatz was one of the city's most prestigious vacant sites, and perhaps that is why people believed the 'Nikeplatz' idea was for real. The centre included elaborate artist's impressions of the 100-foot red swoosh that would dominate the square, and an impressive website too called nikeground.com.

After a flurry of furious letters to the local

papers, the whole enterprise turned out to be an elaborate hoax or – as the perpetrators described it – an arts project. The joke was the brainchild of a radical arts group called 0100101110101101.org, but Nike did not find it amusing.

The trouble was that the Nikeground slogan – 'you want to wear it, why shouldn't cities wear it too?' – sounded all too credible. The significance of the whole business, which went almost unreported outside Austria, wasn't so much the vulnerability of brands to guerrilla arts – that was obvious – but that it went to the heart of why big brands are having a tough time. It seemed somehow obvious that, if Nike could rebrand a much-loved corner of Vienna – or any similar capital city – they probably would have done.

This obvious ambition of the big brands to dominate our mental lives increasingly seems to unnerve people. It is hard to pinpoint precisely where the backlash against brands is coming from, except that politics – in the shape of *No Logo* and the anti-globalisation movement – is really just symptom rather than cause.

Partly the distaste for these monstrous corporate creations is because, as Anita Roddick puts it, they seem unable to experience any other emotions than greed or fear. Partly it is the realisation that artificial food, artificial intelligence, virtual sex, virtual teachers and bank managers are not after all just as good as the real thing. Or the disturbing sense that behind the shiny, jolly logos, there are often miserable sweatshops making Winnie-the-Pooh bags, where the underpaid workers are banned from going to the lavatory. But most of all, it is the creeping exhaustion that comes with dealing with constant manipulation. Almost every public discourse, from magazines to television news, is subtly attempting to cajole, shame or fool us into some kind of action, and we want a break.

If you are rich enough you can avoid it – the US cable channel HBO has no advertisements; McDonalds is banned from the Bahamas. The rest of us get tired of having our defences up all the time. So as a result of the backlash, anti-brands like Muji or Uniqlo have emerged to give the impression that they are somehow more authentic. Yet still the annual surveys by Interbrand show a consistent fall in brand value among the biggest brands. Last year Ford, Disney, AOL, Coca-Cola and Microsoft continued their slow decline.

They respond by swooping on local brands – anything from micro-breweries to local TV channels – and battling each other (as HSBC and

Interbrew did) for the right to call themselves 'The World's Local...'. But still the minority revolt against what is fake, spun, mass-produced and manipulated continues. Very quietly, they are driving the rise of farmers markets, slow food, real ale, reading groups, organic vegetables, poetry recitals, complementary medicine, unbranded fashions and much else besides.

Somehow even the 'Citizen Brand' trend, important as it is, is unable to slow this process. International brands are rootless almost by definition, and that makes their efforts on behalf of real communities and people worldwide carry less conviction.

"Authenticity," wrote the marketing writer Seth Godin: "If you can fake that you can do anything." But authenticity is notoriously difficult to fake, especially for brands – which are polyglot, glitzy, shiny constructs run by shadowy people in distant boardrooms. They have no depth by definition. When you interact with them, you do so with a computer programme – either operated in a call centre or behind the counter by a salesperson who is the frustrated slave of a rationalised delivery system.

The branding think-tank known as the Medinge Group has recognised the basic problem that brands must become "more human and more humane" or they will fail. Humanity is indeed the essence of authenticity, and it is why the big brands have such difficulty meeting this demand. They are one-dimensional non-human approximations.

Kieron O'Hara's recent book *Trust* points out that the core function of brands is to develop a sense of authenticity, and therefore trust. "Brands hold reputations, and that gives the consumer power in the economy," he writes. But this fails to recognise how the very ubiquity of brands, the sheer effort behind their will to win, also now undermines trust – because it isn't really human.

So it isn't somehow that corporate brands – brands as distinguished from simple reputations of organisations – are morally wrong. Or that consumers have changed. It is that they have shouted so loud, so cleverly and so all-pervasively, that they are increasingly useless as generators as trust. So as conventional branding loses its edge because it seems de-humanised, it is not surprising that the word 'community' – a collection of humans – is emerging as the crux of the matter.

Our attitude to 'community' has changed almost 180 degrees over the past half century or so. It is still possible to hear elderly people describing their dislike of communities – the curtain twitching, the disapproval, the stuffy restrictions. But the twenty-first century, exhausted by a culture without roots, longs for community – or at least some sense of it. Even television, which some social critics blame for destroying our social lives, has to respond – and has done, judging by the success of series like *Friends*.

Actually, ersatz community has been at the heart of branding philosophy for some time: the idea that by sharing a logo, you join some kind of enthusiastic virtual group. Like so much else in conventional branding philosophy, this is fantasy, but that is not quite the end of the story.

Where brands have been able to use the concept of community more successfully has been by providing a venue for genuine communities to coalesce. Like Starbucks, which linked up with the Conversation Café movement that began in Seattle. Or the pub chain J. D. Wetherspoons, one of the fastest growing companies in Britain, which adds to their creation of user communities with an individualistic sense of place.

But the most successful 'community brands', in this sense, are those that are not conventional profit-making ventures. Linux, the open source software, is the product of a virtual community of de-buggers, and is increasingly eating into Microsoft's market share – the number of server computers loaded with Linux is growing at 50 per cent a year. That community at its heart is actually one of the main sources of its trust.

Perhaps this also explains the sense of authenticity around an internet giant with no genuine geographical roots at all: eBay. Like Google, eBay is fast, accurate, doesn't overwhelm you with selling messages, and treats you like a real person, rather than a selling opportunity. Like Amazon, they deliberately eschew traditional aspects of branding, spending their money on the service itself. Like Starbucks, they simply provide a venue for new communities, and a highly-efficient search engine that you can use however you want. eBay simply provides a system whereby people can interact. But with eBay, Google and Starbucks alike, it is the customers themselves who are creating the experience. There is no hype and no glitz. Yet eBay now has 48 million users, 430,000 of whom earn most or all of their income selling through the site.

These are not 'community brands' in the sense that they are themselves communities. But they do enable community to evolve, and somehow manage to do so as a by-product of their core business.

The dot.com era was committed to the idea of virtual communities, communities of interest, as if they were somehow just as genuine as real geographical communities. But that always missed the point. Neither eBay nor Google has geographical roots. Starbucks do in the sense that they have a bricks and mortar presence, but they are otherwise ubiquitous and therefore rootless. In the end, communities are at their most authentic when they are 'real' ones somewhere on the map, and it is clear that we no longer quite see it the dot.com way. In fact, over half the British population now lives within a 30 minute journey of where they were born.

This probably has more to do with house prices, and the need to have parents on hand to look after children if both partners need to go out to work. But it is not exactly globalisation, and it is not entirely unwelcome to people who are searching for roots, whether they are psychological, genealogical or historical.

So there is another category of community brands that are designed to provide some aspects of the local. Slow Food, for example, is a brand despite itself. It will never open a shop, or sell you anything except books, yet its membership of over 60,000 and its increasingly influential defence of 'real' food, has given it brand status. Not perhaps on its own account, but as a portal for a range of geographically distinct, local and seasonal foods. Its very logo – the snail, taken from a 1607 food book – demonstrates the rising importance of historical roots along with the geographical ones.

Champagne, Stilton or Parma ham are already local brands, with authentic roots in the past, and now protected by the EU. Slow Food provides a means to revere a whole range of others: Siennese pigs, Vesuvian apricots, Pietmontese cows – real in a way packaged international brands can never be. You will find a similar phenomenon if you go into Neal's Yard Dairy, for example. Or the new store brand launched in Richmond in London called Source – slogan: 'real food for real people'.

It is true that these cater for the upper end of the market, but the geographical roots are clear: every product is labelled according to precisely where it has come from. As the demand starts to grow for fresh, local food – and the success of farmers markets is testament to that – these small food brands, absolutely rooted geographically, will be making themselves much more apparent.

And the portals that make them available, like Source, will be 'community' brands in their own right. Even the new Sainsbury's stores have a string of stalls where you can tailor and have cooked precisely the food you want: it has a whiff of the same thing. Like Slow Food, and like Google in a sense – though not like Sainsbury's – these are brands that eschew their own importance. They step back from the limelight and provide a simple gateway to the local roots we demand.

They are also 'bottom-up' brands. Lynda Gratton's book *The Democratic Enterprise* urges companies to abandon their command-and-control management techniques. The same principle can be applied to brands – they work more effectively, carry more conviction, if they grow out of a very local reality, instead of the shiny constructs imposed from the centre.

One of the obvious symptoms of demands for authenticity has been the way companies are rowing backwards from the Coca-Cola ideal – exactly the same everywhere – to one where every package tells a story of its own. Café Direct has pictures of some of their growers. Some crisp companies give the name of the fryer that made the packet. Lush packaging even has a picture of the employee who made the box. These mini-stories are the stuff of authenticity: the real people and the real places – communities in a way – that made them. Companies that can't tell stories, because the people who made their products are semi-slaves in dingy sweatshops, are at an increasing disadvantage.

None of these 'community brand' categories quite manage to be a community. Google, Starbucks and eBay create communities of interest, but no geographical roots. Slow Food and Neal's Yard create a sense of geographical roots, but no real community. But they are all brands that have a sense of authenticity because of their ability to connect people with what is authentic, or with each other.

It hardly needs saying that it is hard to pin down this glimmer of light that remains for branding. For one thing, the ingenuity of marketing guarantees that there will be other ways of injecting authenticity into your image – or seeming to. For another, communities are awkward places, difficult to live in sometimes, certainly inconvenient.

But you can point to four ways in which you can tell a genuine 'community brand' from one that won't make it. Those that will succeed will:

- Eschew glitz and rationalised delivery systems, and garner trust partly by telling simple stories, partly by their resolute ability to wander off-message.

- Connect with what is human – either because the brand is an expression of a single personality, or because it reveals the personalities of the range of people behind it, or because the service is genuinely personal.

- Have genuine roots to a specific place, or provide a portal to ordinary producers or sellers in specific places.

- Allow customers and employees to feel better connected to their own ideals and values (see for example Neil Crofts' new book *Authentic Business*).

What is interesting is that these are not options for conventional big brands, though some are already trying to muscle in on the community-creation business. Microsoft has been setting up mini-trade fairs in airports. Coke has its 'Red Lounge' initiatives, aimed at creating a sense of community among its consumers. But this is a fantasy born of desperate brand managers. It is bound to disappoint, just as HSBC's supposed local roots disappoint when you phone them up and find yourself talking to a computer somewhere in the ether, using software designed for nobody in particular.

Real community has imperfection at its heart – that is why people tend to trust those with the humanity to risk being off-message – and "imperfection carries a story in a way that perfection can only dream about".

I didn't say that. It comes from the manifesto of the Glasgow-based consultancy Erasmus, and I think they are absolutely right – but imperfection is particularly hard to fake.

Everything today is thoroughly modern – or is it?

In the spring of 2006, the arts establishment seemed to discover a united front and put on a series of exhibitions to try to kick-start modernism, including a huge exhibition at the Victoria & Albert Museum. They received huge publicity. This was my response, which appeared in *Town & Country Planning* in May 2006.

It is now over a century since Frederick Winslow Taylor rose from his chair at the United States Hotel in Saratoga in 1903 and read his paper on time and motion that came to dominate so much of the 20th century. His message was the lessons of his experiments as the world's first management consultant in the Bethlehem steel works in Pennsylvania, persuading the workforce to shift to more 'scientific' patterns of work, and rooting out those who refused.

Taylor was an inveterate inventor, and one of his inventions, a shovel that carried the maximum amount that could be heaved without the user getting tired, has become an unofficial symbol of the rationalised management he pioneered.

It could also be a symbol of modernism itself, the 20th century creed which gave us high-rise flats, the international style, and much else besides. And, in the massive new 'Modernism' exhibition at the Victoria and Albert Museum (V&A), Taylor takes his place – alongside the Futurists and the ideologues of Soviet communism – as the father of our predominant design ideology. And to confirm it, there on the wall beside the Taylor display is a replica of Marcel Duchamp's Manhattan snow shovel from 1915, truly a modern art installation.

Enthroning Taylor as one of the key inspirations of modernism is one of the major achievements of the V&A exhibition, and it is confirmed by the 're-discovery' by curator Christopher Wilk of the importance of performance for the early modernists. Rather robotic performance, in fact – typified in 'Factory Whistles, Rails and Tower', written by poet Andrei Gastav, Director of Lenin's Central Institute of Labour, and based on the idea of 'subordinating people to mechanisms'. Taylorist modernism, in fact.

Modernism has often seemed to divide itself into two apparently unrelated traditions – the white, straight world of the artists and architects, and the rationalised world of the administrators and technocrats. But looking back over a century or so of modernism, we can now see how the two relate to each other, and a little more about why an ideology based on the pursuit of truth should have had such a devastating effect on the places we live – from the heroic glass stumps to the rationalised box systems that now pass for homes.

This debate is worth having again now because London has suddenly gone modernism mad. Not only is there the V&A's massive exhibition, there is also a major show at the Tate Modern about the modernist giants Josef Albers and László Moholy-Nagy. The chattering classes have embraced the exhibitions. The *Guardian* has produced a special supplement. The magazines have been filled with exhibition previews, with background interviews of people who claim to enjoy living in Trellick Towers.

Somehow, the attention given to these people rather gives the game away: the buildings they live in have become symbols of alienation and failure;

the idea that anyone should actually want to live there is newsworthy.

The V&A exhibition is full of black and white photos of pioneering 'machines for living in', in Le Corbusier's phrase. But putting them in the context of the original ideals of modernism – sweeping away the compromised truths that led to war in 1914, the thrill of speed and machinery, the revelation of the machinery of the human body – does provide some insights into why it all proved so disappointing.

Misunderstanding humanity

First, modernism misunderstood humanity. "The old human spirit is invalidated and in flux towards a new form," said Bauhaus founder Walter Gropius, and his words are etched in giant letters over the exhibition.

In practice, most of the pictures of people at the V&A exhibition are idealised, serious, athletic types. The only smiles are in a 1935 film called *Housing Problem*, on people in crumbling terraced housing somewhere in industrial Britain, with their outside lavatories and taps (houses which have probably long since been taken over by lawyers with vast mortgages).

It makes you wonder, comparing the sad

uniformity of the ideal – pictures of solemn modernist types doing mass demonstrations of gymnastics – with the evident enjoyment of the old, whether Gropius threw the baby out with the old human spirit's bathwater.

Yet between the lines in the Tate Britain exhibition, there is some evidence that the 'old human spirit' survives after all – rather inconveniently (as it does) – even for the crowned kings of modernism. Despite shunning decoration and colour on behalf of Bauhaus, Albers remained obsessed with both for the rest of his life. As for Moholy-Nagy, the pictures of his trade-mark balconies – even in his own flat – show them adapted in a very human way for his children, with some pieces of very unmodernist chicken wire. I regard this as a hopeful sign. People are not quite herdable after all.

Misunderstanding efficiency
Then there was the way the modernists came to misunderstand efficiency, which is why they seem to have unceremoniously dumped those aspects of early modernism that sat uneasily with puritanical clean lines: the patterns, the colour, the women and the craft.

Women especially. Looking at the V&A exhibition, I was left wondering why – with the exception of Sonia Delaunay's knitted swimming costume or Marianne Brandt's hand-made teapot – there was so little by women. Just things for them, like the famous pioneering Hamburg time-and-motion kitchen which all the others since have been based on. It is time somebody organised an exhibition about the lost women of modernism. There is a story to be told, and not just Bruno Taut's 1926 remark, picked out in big letters at the V&A, that "women must sweep away domestic nostalgia and make a new beginning".

But the influence of Taylor, among others, provides a clue about why modernism – under either Soviet communism, German fascism or British *nothingverymuchism* – insists on sweeping away everyone's domestic nostalgia. From a modernist standpoint, these individual foibles are just inefficient. But the alternative – only making use of those parts of the human being that can be sublimated to the machine, and wasting the rest – that isn't efficient at all.

Misunderstanding materialism

Then there is the whole business of reality. Take chairs, for example. We know of course, from a century of experience, that some modern chair designs are comfortable and light, while others are like strapping human beings into metal frames. The V&A reminds us of Marcel Breuer's 1926 prediction about chairs that "in the end we will sit on a column of air". The internet guru Nicholas Negraponte now predicts a future he calls "nothing, never, nowhere". The material world remains an inconvenience for serious modernists.

This is really the nub of the issue. Modernism prefers abstraction to reality, machines to human beings, columns of light to flesh and blood; and therein lies its tragedy. Because the former is impossible without the latter. That contradiction explains the deadening results of nearly a century of modernism in practice, obvious in all our towns and cities. And since that tension was present even in the original ideals, I can't help feeling it was inevitable.

Cheap, regimented and standardised
So I am suspicious – or curious at least – about why we are being force-fed modernism again by the arts establishment at this critical stage in the new century. The reason, hinted at the end of the V&A exhibition, is this: modernism is now, as the V&A puts it, a "symbol of global capitalism".

Actually, it is worse than that. Whatever its

idealistic origins, modernism is now the preferred language of the rich and powerful. It underpins the ethic of technocracy, because it is cheap, regimented, standardised and ubiquitous. It disapproves of awkward individuality. It is no longer really compatible with human beings, and their awkward corners, if indeed it ever was. So when the establishment decides that modernism needs a few monkey glands to keep it alive a little longer, they organise an exhibition at the V&A and get the chattering classes marvelling once more over the simplicity and cleanliness of it all.

It is time that the establishment realised the game is up. It's over. The trouble is, they don't get it yet. London's modernist mayor (Livingstone) is still peddling monstrous glass shards across the city, in the international style, without history, culture or humanity – diminishing all those who have to live round them. The Deputy Prime Minister (Prescott), while also First Secretary of State, along with elements of the architectural lobby, promoted a new generation of system-built hutches for the poor, in miserable high-density suburbs. Public service managers are promoting rationalised systems that provide learning outcomes instead of education, or units of intervention instead of healthcare.

These are all the children of modernism. They share the same gap between appearance and reality, between 'columns of air' and awkward human individuality.

I am not one of those who believe the arts are irrelevant to modern life. Quite the reverse: these misunderstandings matter. We need our cultural institutions to start re-examining the accepted truths of modernism. Does an international style, shorn of its human, cultural and historical roots, really benefit our cities – or does it impoverish them? Was there ever anything to the idea of 'progress', the modernist incantation that could justify any abomination in the 1960s and 1970s? Did it mean anything except 'change'?

It may be that we were intended to ask just these questions at the V&A, but the rather weak affirmation at the end of the show – that modernism "remains relevant to the 21st century" – rather suggests not.

After the blind alley

Another question we ought to examine is this: now modernism has led us up such a blind alley, what is coming next? I don't mean post-modernism, which is simply a confused child of its parent – giving us irony instead of depth – but rather the fascination with the human spirit that seems dimly to be emerging to take the place of the great machine creed.

So let me make a few predictions about the next decade. We will not see a revival of revitalised modernism, but an increasingly powerful rejection of that kind of standardisation – in politics, planning and architecture. We will see *salons des refusées* for artists who dare again to seek out beauty and meaning, when the establishment insists that they produce ironic video performances or sail wooden huts down rivers. We will see a widespread revival of the authentic – real food, real shops, face-to-face management, medicine and education with real relationships at their heart, and human-scale buildings and diverse shopping streets with the local details the international style has done so much to excise – because that is what people demand.

We will look back on the early years of the 21st century, not for lovingly rediscovering the ethics of modernism that helped render the previous century inhuman, but for the first glimmerings of the philosophy – a different attempt at truth – that replaces it.

What that implies for places is not clear, except that we will demand their authenticity, just as the places we exist in now shimmer on the edge of shiny, ubiquitous, modernist unreality. The new ethic will be recognisable by depth. These will not be shiny one-dimensional approximations of cities, food and management: they will be human, three-dimensional reality, rooted in history and culture. Yes, we will struggle to find ways of providing this in a multi-cultural society, where any cultural depth risks parochial intolerance, but we will find it in our shared but different humanity.

We might then look back on this decade with some astonishment, as our government plunged into hideous mistakes – Iraq, NHS rationalisation – because of a complete ignorance of history. We will wonder how we ever unravelled ourselves from an architectural and political establishment that – as Talleyrand said of the Bourbons – forgets nothing and remembers nothing. Fingers crossed that we do.

So go along to the V&A exhibition if you get the chance. It is like the watching the great leviathans of Dickensian art at the Royal Academy ignoring the emergence of Degas and Monet in France. It is the last gasp of the philosophy that has dominated the creation of places almost since this magazine was founded a century ago, and which this magazine has been almost alone in resisting, through the high-rise era and beyond.

It will be nice to be able to tell your grandchildren that you were there to see the last gasp of the monster.

The new authenticity

This essay was published in 2011 in *The Palgrave Handbook of Spirituality and Business*, and it responds to the prevailing critique of the authenticity agenda – that it is, as two American authors put it: 'fake, fake, fake'. That is the state of the prevailing argument about authenticity – is it a delusion that must be satisfied or is there still something that people are searching for?

I used to explain my decision, sometime around 2001, to write a book about the growing demand for authenticity, by telling the story of a dinner party. A friend of mine had told us why he had bought a flat in Paris. It was, he said, "because they have real shops there". Thinking about it afterwards, I realised that this was not 'real' in any of its conventional definitions, yet everyone knew immediately what he meant.

He meant tiny, colourful, family-owned stores, full of evocative smells and baking on the premises, in neighbourhoods where the customers might be known by name by the shopkeeper.

This was more evidence for me that something peculiar was happening to the word 'real', not for everybody but among enough of us to matter. Although most people I talked to about this seemed to be unable to define exactly what they meant by 'authentic', they knew what it was when we saw it, whether it was real food, real culture, real politics, real schools, real community, real medicine or real stories. There was something, apparently indefinable, which held these things together.

This was bound to be anecdotal research. But it was clear to me that, whatever people meant by 'authentic', they did not mean it in the sense that Freud or Marx might have meant it, or even as Coca-Cola or Ralph Lauren might have meant it either. The business of Coca-Cola's Dasani bottled water, which actually came from the main water supply, underlined the fact that there was some tension going on here. The tension was all the clearer when you realised that the same brand name shirts being made in the Far Eastern factories which were also churning out the fakes.

Paul Ray suggested that the 'cultural creatives' phenomenon in the USA included about a quarter of the American population. This seems to be a parallel but related idea. Ray said that cultural creatives believed themselves to be almost alone in the definitions and tastes, shared just by themselves and a few friends railing against the world, when it was actually a much more widely shared understanding. This is likely to apply also to the new definition of 'real'. There is actually a sizeable minority who use the word 'authentic' in this new way, as part of a growing revolt against what was fake, spun, mass-produced and manipulated. Very quietly, and below the radar of the cultural commentators – except perhaps for a few – this is what had been driving the rise of farmers' markets, slow food, real ale, reading groups, organic vegetables, poetry recitals, complementary medicine, unbranded fashions, and much else besides.

The demand for what is real is obvious from the packaging in shops, and in the world of advertising, where there are constant appeals to authenticity, often to obscure the fact that the product is deeply inauthentic in some way. Looking at food packets, it is clear that real is now also a slightly atavistic reaction against some aspects of technological hope. Despite all those predictions by technocrats and globalisers, we are not taking our food in pill form as we were told we would. We haven't had the genius machines, able to think for themselves (predicted in 1970). Or human embryo packets in shops (1966). Or robots to look after the elderly (1983). Or the disappearance of kitchens (1970). Or artificial moons instead of street-lighting (1968). We haven't handed over our futures to virtual teachers or doctors, though clearly that remains a possibility.

The combination of all these factors represents a demand for food that tastes of something, does not involve the genes of fish for temperature control or human hair to make the dough stretchy, and comes from a real place somewhere on the map. Far from losing our regional identities in a global world, half of the UK population now lives within a thirty-minute journey of where they were born. To describe the contemporary world as 'globalised' clearly is not entirely accurate.

An estimated twelve million Europeans are now downshifting by cutting salary or hours in search of more 'authentic' living. Another two million have given up the rat race entirely. And we are seeing the slow decline of the big brands like McDonald's and Coca-Cola as they desperately portray themselves as 'local'. When I was writing the book, HSBC and Interbrew – two global giants without local roots or culture – were battling over the legal right to call themselves 'The world's local...'

There is another strand behind the new meaning of the word 'real', and that is where business theory and new age self-improvement meets. One element of this is the emergence of a broad argument about our working lives: that we are likely to be more effective and fulfilled if we are in some sense true to our own natures. There is also an emerging debate about 'authentic leadership' in the corporate world, notably following the survey of leaders by Bill George, CEO of Medtronic, which found that authentic leadership related more to self-reflection and honesty than to any in-born gift. These are different, but related, meanings. They are also a clue about the central argument of authenticity.

It has become increasingly clear to me since in some ways launching this debate, that – when it comes to authenticity in marketing and business – there are essentially two views about all this, and they are broadly about whether authenticity itself is real.

There is a prevailing view among some commentators that takes the opposite view, and you can see why. Authenticity is impossible, they say, because everything is constructed. That means any appeal to authenticity by companies and advertisers must be manipulative. By definition, it is fake. As the social commentator Seth Godin put it: "Authenticity – if you can fake that, the rest will take care of itself."

It is true that advertising and marketing regularly appeals to our insatiable demand for what is real, especially – perhaps inevitably – when the offering is particularly fake. There are now so many overlapping meanings to the word, that almost anybody can claim it for anything – ethical, original, natural, pure. We navigate these claims every day, and actually do so quite easily. Despite the predictions that somehow real and fake would become hopelessly interlinked, we actually distinguish the two without difficulty. We do so particularly on television, where 'reality' – heavily manipulated by producers – is almost all that is on offer. When we feel particularly manipulated, either by the media or politicians, there is a public outcry. The BBC and ITV ended up paying large fines for the way they had manipulated the people answering their premium phone line quiz programmes.

But the marketing of real has moved on as well. Two American business consultants, James

Gilmore and Joseph Pine, published a book, also called *Authenticity*, which was designed as a manual for businesses. It was full of fascinating insights into the way the culture of real is developing. But they share the opinion of many of my original reviewers. "It's all fake, fake, fake," they said. To prove this, they compared Eurodisneyland with the Netherlands and concluded that both were equally constructed landscapes. All businesses can do is to successfully give the impression of authenticity, "so that people may perceive them as real, real, real".

They advised, helpfully, that "it is easier to be authentic if you don't say you're authentic", and "if you say you're authentic, then you'd better be authentic".

This is a similar point of view to the arguments posed against the idea of 'authentic tourism'. If authentic means somehow unpackaged, or unreplicable, they argue that this is a meaningless concept.

That is quite right, but there is a contradiction here. If everything is 'fake, fake, fake', how can any business possibly *be* authentic? The problem is that using post-modern tools to deconstruct the idea – and discovering, of course, that nothing is real – rather misses the key point. The demand for authenticity is itself a critique of the prevailing postmodern culture. It is a demand for authenticity in the face of this hopeless relativism, accepting it but moving on beyond it. It is an ongoing search for what holds people together despite their atomisation by postmodern culture, endlessly deconstructed into their own distant silos. "In an unreal world, people long for reality even more," wrote the American philosopher Robert Nozick, and that is what is happening here.

My sense is that the most enthusiastic doyens of authenticity are not expecting some kind of platonic ideal. They know that the ground shifts in terms of what is possible all the time. What they are looking for is evidence of effort, of ideals, of truth, of passion – anything which shows the business they are dealing with is a collection of human beings, rooted in human tradition, and not a shiny one-dimensional construct. In short, what holds people together in a post-postmodern world is our common humanity. This is a flawed possibility. It is hopeful and decaying and weather-beaten, and it is all this that makes it real. Real means human.

We have moved beyond the definition of authentic set out by the sociologist Lionel Trilling in terms of what it is not – not from mankind, not mechanical and not monetary. Of course, real can still mean natural and unadulterated, but the new meaning primarily means something to do with human connection – it is, in some ways, the reverse. That is the clue provided by the literature about authentic work and authentic leadership. It would be incoherent to suggest that business leaders should fake their authentic leadership.

The other evidence that real is *real* is that, despite the huge difficulties of providing authenticity to a mass market, mainstream business is responding. Linux, the open source software, is the product of a virtual community of de-buggers, and has been increasingly eating into Microsoft's market share, partly because it has a community of committed human beings at its heart. Other successful corporations in the age of authenticity try to stand back and let people use them in whatever way they want, whether it is eBay or Starbucks. "Mass advertising can help build brands, but authenticity is what makes them last," said Starbucks CEO Howard Schultz. eBay simply provides a system whereby people can interact. Like Google and Starbucks, it is the customers themselves who are creating the experience.

But there is no doubt it is tough for the big

corporate world, which inevitably longs to cut the costs of dealing with ordinary human beings, to provide a human service of any kind. They are up against a plethora of tiny, but authentic competitors, eating away at their market share. The micro-breweries and micro-publishers, the niche food producers and the local services, which provide products from somewhere in particular, often with the name of the person – for example, who fried the crisps – printed on the packet. Café Direct has pictures of some of their growers. Lush packaging even has a picture of the employee who made the box.

It is hardly surprising that the micro-breweries are being snapped up by the big brands, and the big publishers are launching new imprints that look and feel like self-publishing. Kelloggs are even lampooning the whole idea by printing a picture of the old lady on their Shreddies packets who they pretend knitted the shreddies in the pack. These human stories are the very stuff of authenticity: the real people and the real places that made them. Companies that can't tell stories, because the people who made their products are semi-slaves in dingy sweatshops, are at an increasing disadvantage.

Authenticity is not quite the same as ethics. It is

possible to be an ethical company without seeming in the least authentic. You can be ethical and still deliver everything virtually. But ethics are a signal that a company or organisation is more than its image. It is a sign that it has human depth.

In some ways, these very failures are a sign that a company is somehow real. Real companies have imperfection at their heart. That is why people tend to trust those with the humanity to risk being off-message. "Imperfection carries a story in a way that perfection can only dream about," said a Glasgow-based consultancy called Erasmus in their manifesto. I think they are absolutely right, and imperfection is particularly hard to fake.

On the other hand, there clearly is an ethical dimension to authenticity too. It represents a critique of the way mainstream business operates, as it distances customers from human reality, replacing human interaction with software or compulsory script. Despite their protestations of humanity, so many companies still plunge callers into call centre hell. These are particularly sharp issues for organisations, public and private, that are delivering public services, and believing they can do so increasingly virtually. It is also an issue for organisations which try to control every decision, reaction and detailed inter-reaction of their staff, which is the other side of the same coin.

People feel, without even perhaps articulating it, that there is something sinister about this combination. Not perhaps when you try to communicate with a call centre or website that omits your particular request on its software. That is merely irritating. But when you need those services, or when they dominate your lives – like immigration authorities – then fakeness can be terrifying.

Of course, it would be frightening if you are on a long-term care ward in a hospital that is only interested in Whitehall targets, and will sacrifice you and your fellow patients to achieve them. Or if you have applied for citizenship, and handed over your passport some years before to the immigration authorities, and you are trapped in the country without paperwork, without being able to visit your parents abroad, and with no answer from the bureaucracy as the years go by.

When we go through the great portals of a modern corporation, whether it is public or private, past the disapproving eyes of those with the power to let you in the gate, we know deep down that we are entering – not just a fake world – but an almost Soviet one. It is a world of empire and obscure politics, where hierarchy, control and bizarre distorted information has a huge effect on the lives of the people who work there or depend on it. That kind of hierarchical system eventually collapsed under its own internal contradictions in Eastern Europe.

We are victims when we work for these systems, and when the pointlessness of another questionnaire on another obscure government target suddenly hits us in the morning as we go to work. But there are bigger victims too, from those whose medical treatment is constrained because of obscure rules based on the cost effectiveness of the treatment to other people, to the eleven-year-olds drilled into dullness on summer afternoons to pass the multiple choice questions on the SATS.

The symbol of this problem was the poor repairman from the American cable giant Comcast, who fell asleep during a routine home call at the home of a man called Brian Finkelstein in 2006. Finkelstein filmed him snoring and stuck it online, together with the sound track of a song called 'I need some sleep'. The repairman was fired. But it transpired that he had actually fallen asleep after waiting over an hour on the phone to get through the useless call centre at his own useless office.

This is an extension of the whole question of

authenticity, which has so far concentrated mainly on products – whether they are food or politicians. There is a parallel problem about services and public institutions, which have become progressively hollowed out by a combination of inappropriate IT, command-and-control call centres and 'rationalised' systems that exclude the human element.

The result is that our institutions are often now empty shells, shorn of human emotions and connection, echoing spaces where human values and intricacy ought to be, and prey to the fantasy of efficiency which has corroded them. Actually, organisations which exclude human relationships are probably less effective, more inefficient, more expensive and more prone to huge mistakes than those which encourage them. That is the side-effect of fake.

Authenticity is bound to be a slippery concept. It is particularly slippery if we leave it to the marketing departments and business academics. The point is that, behind it, is a real demand, a real need and a series of real fears, that are important – and especially important now in the next phase of the development of effective organisations, from schools to hospitals, from police stations to justice systems.

Authenticity is not just a vague marketing whim. It is a tool by which we can begin to analyse the failures and successes of our institutions.

The book I was discussing here was: James H. Gilmore and Joseph Pine (2007), Authenticity: What consumers really want, Harvard Business School Press, Cambridge.

Afterthought
The lunch, the cook
and the larder

I was commissioned to write this article by a government agency which wanted to explore, in interesting new ways, some of the current dilemmas about food. Perhaps, in retrospect, it was always obvious that they would not dare publish it. It was published instead in the first edition of the online newsletter *Ethical Junction* in February 2007. We still have pretty much the same dilemmas now, and most are related to authenticity. Sprockett's Farm was a reference to a scene at the end of the Ealing Studios comedy *Kind Hearts and Coronets* (another post-modern cultural reference – it is hard to quite give them up).

Once there were four children whose names were Peter, Susan, Edmund and Lucy. They lived with an old professor in the countryside, and they were bored. Or rather Edmund was bored. He was sitting in the school playground (safety regulation: no running) and complaining about the lunch.

"It's always the same," he said. "Turkey dinosaurs fried with mango and pineapple. Every Tuesday. And I read it's the same for 44 per cent of the world: they all get fried turkey dinosaurs on a Tuesday in those same self-heating plastic packs made by Coca-Cargill Unilever. And guess how much it costs: 17p each. 'Economies of scale', they call it. I call it disgusting."

"How can you be bored, again, Edmund?" said Lucy. "My Gran says that, when she was at school, all they got was peas, potatoes and cabbage. Now we get chicken alphabets and passionfruit jelly from a squeezable tube – on Wednesdays, anyway."

"Potatoes! That would be something! We never get those any more."

Sadly for the children, only one form of potato had been approved by the European Union for cultivation and it had caught a virulent blight and died out. There had been a heritage seeds project, burying unapproved varieties under the Arctic icecap for posterity, but the Arctic icecap was no more.

"But we get Nu-potato. That's nearly as good. When we went to the TescoVirgin store last week, they had so many varieties of Nu-potato. Blue, pink, purple, green. That's choice, isn't it."

"But it's all the same gut-churner underneath," said Edmund bitterly.

"Some people are never satisfied," said Susan, sucking a Taste Pill™. She looked out across the dense undergrowth of what had once been Sprockett's Farm and the hyper-highway in the distance.

"Don't you think it's romantic? Look at those TescoVirgin trucks. They're bringing in our milk all the way from Ukraine. Think what they've seen!" She took a long swig from their bottle of water, guaranteed free from fertiliser or additives. The professor refused to let them drink from the tap.

"TescoVirgin, TescoVirgin! That's the only company we ever hear about. I think they make everything!"

"You know that's not true," said Peter, who read the business-sport pages every morning. "There's Coca-Cargill Unilever as well, isn't there."

"Yes and the water I'm drinking," added Susan. "Look at the slogan: 'Your Clean Local Water'."

"Actually, it's a subsidiary of TescoVirgin. It's

just bottled here," said Peter. "All British companies are part of TescoVirgin now. They had to be big to compete with Coca-Cargill Unilever. That means more competition."

"Yes, and competition is good for the economy," said Susan. "Miss Leahy says so. And we need to be able to earn enough to buy flowers every year." Britain's wild flowers had unfortunately been contaminated by Terminator seed technology and died out in the space of a season, leaving the bushes bare. Public-spirited people like the professor invest in new plants from South Africa every year to try and keep the colour in the countryside.

The food they eat is a source of lesson plans for Miss Leahy, though the professor grinds his teeth when he hears about it. They have school debates about whether the sachets of British horseradish (Hungarian horseradish, acetic acid and Polish cream) they get on Mondays are really British. But then, if the school only has to spend 17p per lunch, they can afford an extra teacher and more books. And since that extra teacher is Miss Leahy, she is quite keen on the status quo.

It's sad about the farms, but there's always Farm World Theme Park™, which Peter and Susan are particularly keen on. You get to see real cows – well, one of them – real tractors and pat the sheep, who lead an idyllic existence of stroking, fed by the most delicious-tasting Chinese agricultural meal, with seven different tastes, one for each day of the week. And although the price of food is rising rather worryingly – it is now very dependent on oil prices – there is still the most exotic series of choices in TescoVirgin. It's so exciting going in the doors and encountering again the recorded smell of baking bread – mmm, delicious!

Edmund was in the Behaviour stream at school (dissent was a discipline issue). Peter, Susan and Lucy were in the Asthma stream. It seemed sensible to organise the classes that way, so that medical staff could maximise their time and vigilance in the right places.

After school, the four friends joined the supervised walk down the high street, with its shuttered abandoned shops, to the delights of TescoVirgin. "I can't think why Edmund's always so bored," said Peter, shaking his wise old head ...

*

That night, Edmund was not just bored – he was hungry. He crept downstairs to the professor's old-fashioned larder: the professor shunned the new computerised kitchen-larders which automatically dialled TescoVirgin when anything was finished. The professor's larder even smelled old-fashioned.

Peter muttered about botulism, but Edmund loved its smell of long-mislaid cheese.

There it was again, as he surveyed the shelves for something to eat. But his eye was attracted instead to a hole behind the fridge he had never seen before. He peered inside, pushed past the old tea-towels and crawled further in.

It really was the longest larder, but suddenly he found himself in a small clump of grass. To his astonishment, it was sunny. He stood up and looked around. There were wild-flowers everywhere, and the unmistakable noise of a tractor.

A terrifying lady in white stood before him glaring: the tallest lady he'd ever seen, proud and cold. "Who are you?" he said, before he could stop himself.

"I'm the school cook," she said.

"We don't have a cook, do we?" The school cook just glared.

"Well, I'm glad to run into you because I'm ever so hungry," said Edmund. "I could even eat fried Nu-potato. But I'd prefer a pineapple or mandarin."

"Oh, we don't have those any more," said the cook. "We haven't done since the great oil price hike, don't you remember – or were you too young? Let me see, it's autumn now. I can get you some delicious apples, grown at Sprockett's Farm."

"That overgrown dump?"

Not only was Sprockett's not overgrown, it was a hive of activity, divided into three separate holdings, funded by a local customers who paid a subscription for a vegetable and fruit box every week, which they picked up from the local school.

Edmund followed the cook down the high street, and his eyes nearly popped out of his head as he looked at the little shops there, with their striped awnings.

Some were selling local cheeses in an array of rather frightening colours. Others were selling fruit. There was even one shop selling greeting cards: a poster in the window said: 'Happy Apple Season! Make your day especially scrunchy!'

But something was missing: where was the vast red-brick structure with no windows?

"Where's TescoVirgin?"

"I seem to remember there was something like that," said the cook. "Have you come from another planet? When the oil prices rose, and people wanted healthier food, they broke up the big companies. I know the farmers are all millionaires now, and there are no bananas, but it's a small price to pay."

"No bananas? I don't believe you."

"Well, there are bananas of course, but you have to buy them in the West End. I can't afford them myself."

They were now at the school gates and the cook led him inside. "Come along," she said. "I'll make you something to eat, as long as no-one's looking."

Inside the school kitchen – which Edmund was sure used to be the staff room – there were boxes marked Sprockett's Farm, and other farms with place names within the radius of 20 miles or so, all piled up to the ceiling."

"Where are the turkey dinosaurs?"

"What! Those horrors were banned years back, and a good thing too. No, we only buy organic local food. We have to: the governors decided. Just like the hospital up the road: they're the same."

"How fantastic!"

"Fantastic, nothing," said the cook, with a bitter expression. "I have to chop all these things myself – the only help I ever get is when one of the children is in detention. And some of the veg they send me – well, it should have been fed to the pigs if you ask me.

"When I was a girl we got our food from all over the world. Now you're lucky if you can get a parsnip from the other side of Birmingham."

Edmund didn't like to ask what a parsnip was, so he excused himself. "I'd better go back and find my friends. They're in the Asthma stream."

"Asthma?" said the cook. "Never heard of it."

*

As he made his way quickly back home, he remembered disconcerting stories about people who had slipped into other worlds and found that centuries had gone by. He began to run.

He found the clump of grass again and squeezed inside, past the tea-towels, but he emerged – not in the professor's magic larder, with Peter, Susan and Lucy sleeping upstairs – but in a large expanse of tarmac. Where was he?

Then he saw in the dark ahead of him, a sign he could just read: it said 'TescoVirgin: disabled parking only'.

"I can't believe it," said Edmund to himself. "They've concreted over the professor. Now I'll never get back home."

From Scandal: How homosexuality became a crime

Also published by The Real Press, available in print and as an ebook (see www.therealpress.co.uk).

It was Saturday 6 April 1895. The weather was windy and drizzly as the passengers packed onto the quayside at Dover to catch the steam packet to Calais, due on the evening tide. Perhaps it was packed that night because of Easter the following week. Perhaps it wasn't as packed as some of the witnesses claimed later, or the downright gossips who weren't actually there. But it was still full. Those waiting on the quay wrapped up warm against the chilly Channel breeze and eyed each other nervously, afraid to meet anyone they knew, desperately wanting to remain anonymous.

Among those heading for France that night was an American, Henry Harland, the editor and co-founder of the notorious quarterly known as *The Yellow Book*, the journal of avant garde art and writing which had taken England by the scruff of the neck in the 1890s. Harland had come to Europe with his wife Aline, pretending to have been born in St Petersburg and planning to live in Paris, but had instead made his London flat, at 144 Cromwell Road, the very hive of excitement in the literary world. Henry James, Edmund Gosse and Aubrey Beardsley came and went. The parties were talked about with awe and excitement. Henry and Aline always spent the spring in Paris, so they were not leaving the country suddenly and in desperation, but it dawned on them that the reason the quayside was so packed that night was because many others were.

The name of the ferry the Harlands boarded has been lost to history. It was probably the *Victoria* – her sister ship the *Empress* had been badly damaged in a collision the month before and was now in dry dock. There she heaved beside the sea wall, as the muffled passengers filed up the gangway, her twin rakish masts and her twin funnels belching smoke, her two paddlewheels poised to drive across the world's busiest sea lane at 18 knots, her stern flag flapping in the wind with the insignia of the London, Chatham and Dover Railway.

Harland had a good idea why the ferries were

full, though he was still surprised. He was also aware of at least some of the implications for himself. Oscar Wilde had been arrested for 'gross indecency' that evening, having lost his libel action the day before. The news of the warrant for his arrest was in the evening papers, and included the information that Wilde had been arrested while he had been reading a copy of *The Yellow Book* (this was quite wrong, in fact; he was reading *Aphrodite* by Pierre Louys). Harland could only guess the motivations of those who were now suddenly crowding across the English Channel, but it looked remarkably like fear. They huddled in corners in the stateroom downstairs, out of the wind, damp and smuts, wondering perhaps whether they would ever see their native land again.

There was an unnerving atmosphere of menace that evening. One item in the evening papers implied that the nation was perched on the edge of a scandal that would make the establishment teeter. "If the rumours which are abroad tonight are proved to be correct we shall have such an exposure as has been unheard of in this country for many years past."

Did it mean the exposure would reach those who run the nation, or did it mean something even more terrifying – that the exposure would spread downwards through society? As the passengers knew only too well, the combination of events which they had feared for a decade had now come to pass. It had been a few months short of ten years since the so-called 'Labouchère amendment' had been rushed through the House of Commons, criminalising homosexual activity of any kind between men. It was never quite clear why women were excluded – there is no evidence for the old story that Queen Victoria claimed it was impossible. For ten years now, they had watched the rising sense of outrage at the very idea of 'homosexuality' – though the term was not yet in common use – and had realised that there might come a time when that law was enforced with an unsurpassed ferocity.

It wasn't that they necessarily had anything to be ashamed of – quite the reverse – but they had reputations to be lived down, some event in their past or some 'unfortunate' relationship behind them. Now that public concern had turned

to what looked like public hysteria, they clearly had to be vigilant. They did not want to be accused, as Oscar Wilde was accused, by a violent aristocrat of doubtful sanity, and would then have to respond in the courts or the press. They could not face the fatal knock on the front door from a smiling acquaintance who would turn out to be a dangerous blackmailer.

But now the unthinkable had happened. Wilde had been stupid enough to sue the Marquess of Queensberry for libel, and had lost. The public had driven each other into a crescendo of rage and it seemed only sensible to lie low in Paris for a while. Or Nice or Dieppe, or the place where the British tended to go in flight from the law – Madrid. Anywhere they could be beyond the reach of the British legal system.

As we shall see, one of those who fled, as I discovered during the research that led to this book, was my own great-great-grandfather – escaping for the second time in a just over a decade, in a story that my own family had suppressed for three generations.

It is no small matter to flee your home and go abroad, especially to do so within the space of a few hours to gather your belongings and make arrangements for your property or your money. As it is, escape was only a solution available to those wealthy enough to flee. It is even tougher perhaps for those in some kind of unconventional relationship, ambiguous to the outside world – but perhaps not ambiguous enough – aware that the decision to go was probably irreversible. It might look like an admission of guilt.

On the other hand, what might happen when the newspapers could unleash this kind of bile? What would happen when they had successfully gaoled Wilde with hard labour and turned on his friends, and anyone else who looked unusual? What would happen if the rumours were correct and the scandal would shortly engulf the government and royal family? Harland did not know at this stage that, when the news about *The Yellow Book* became clear on Monday morning, a mob would gather outside the offices of his publishers Bodley Head, and would break all the windows. "It killed *The Yellow Book* and it nearly killed me," said publisher John Lane later.

We know now that, in the event, the threatened conflagration did not take place, but in the remaining 72 years while Section 11 of the Criminal Law Amendment Act, the Labouchère Amendment, stayed on the statute books, 75,000 were prosecuted under its terms, among them John Gielgud, Lord Montagu and Alan Turing. Many thousands of lives were ruined – Turing committed suicide not long afterwards, having been forced to undergo hormone treatment that made him grow breasts.

Yet that moment of fear in Britain in 1895, unprecedented in modern times, has been largely forgotten. It is remembered as a sniggering remnant of gossip, about the number of English aristocrats or others in public life, living incognito in Dieppe, or glimpsed in the bars in Paris, and the awareness as a result that they had something to hide. One of the purposes of this book is to remember it for what it was – one of the most disturbing chapters in modern English history, when public horror at sexual behaviour reached such intensity that nobody seemed completely safe, and nobody could be relied on to protect you. And when a man like Wilde, the darling of the theatre critics, with two sell-out shows in London's West End theatres, could be brought low by a furious, litigious pugilist – well, really, who was safe?

This unique moment of fear in English history came at a peculiar moment, at perhaps the apogee of tolerance in so many other ways – women were cycling and getting university degrees, training to be doctors. Mohandas Gandhi was a London-trained barrister working in South Africa. George Bernard Shaw was overturning assumptions about the right way to dress, eat and spell. H. G. Wells was sleeping his way through the ranks of the young female Fabians. Edward Carpenter, in his sandals, was advertising freedom from the constraints of conventional sexuality, having forged a gay relationship with a working class man from Sheffield. William Morris was still, just, preaching a revolution based on medieval arts and crafts. And yet the rage at the idea that men should love each other sexually threatened to overwhelm everything.

That morning, Queensberry had received a telegram from an anonymous supporter, which read: "Every man in the City is with you. Kill the bugger."

Why did it happen? Partly because of growing public concern following the Labouchère amendment, sneaked though Parliament in 1885, but even that was more than the individual brainchild of a lone radical. Why this shift from tolerance of the changing role of women and emerging new ideas to this threatening public rage? How did homosexuality emerge as a key issue in English public life?

The answer lies in the events that took place in Dublin a decade before, starting with the political aftermath of the murder of Lord Frederick Cavendish, the son of the Duke of Devonshire and the newly-appointed Chief Secretary to Ireland.

But I had a more personal reason for finding out the answers to some of these questions. My family lived in Dublin in the 1880s. The reason that they don't any more, and that I was born in England not Ireland, was because of those same events there in that decade. Until the last few years, when I began researching this book, I was unaware of them.

All I knew was that my great-great-grandfather, the banker Richard Boyle, had left Dublin suddenly and under a cloud around 1884. His photograph has been torn out of the family photo album, with only his forehead remaining. There are no likenesses of him anywhere that I know about. The letters related to these events in the family, and what followed, have long since been destroyed. I believe I was even there when my grandfather burned the last of them on the bonfire around 1975.

I had always been interested in what might have happened, but had assumed that the memories were now beyond recovery, just as the fate of my great-great-grandfather was lost in the mists of unfathomable time.

As it turned out, I was wrong. I was working on another incident in Irish history in the British Library, and discovered as I did so that a whole raft of Victorian Irish newspapers had been digitised and were now searchable online. On an impulse, I put in the name 'Richard Boyle' and searched through the references in the Dublin papers. Then, suddenly, my heart began beating a little faster, because there it was – the first clue I found to a personal tragedy, and a national tragedy too: this was the spark that lit the fuse which led to the criminalisation of gay behaviour and the great moment of fear that followed the arrest of Oscar Wilde.

That first clue led to others, which led to others. I will never know the whole story, but what I did discover took me on a historical rollercoaster, and an emotional one, which catapulted me back to the strangely familiar world of the end of the nineteenth century – and a glimpse of that sudden fear in April 1895 that drove many of those affected so suddenly abroad....

Read more by buying Scandal...

Other titles by David Boyle

Building Futures
Funny Money: In search of alternative cash
What is New Economics?
The Sum of our Discontent
The Tyranny of Numbers
The Money Changers
Numbers (with Anita Roddick)
Authenticity: Brands, Fakes, Spin and the Lust for
Real Life
Blondel's Song
Leaves the World to Darkness (fiction)
News from Somewhere (*editor*)
Toward the Setting Sun
The New Economics: A Bigger Picture (with
Andrew Simms)
Money Matters: Putting the eco into economics
The Wizard
The Little Money Book
Why London Needs its own Currency
Eminent Corporations (with Andrew Simms)
Voyages of Discovery
The Human Element
On the Eighth Day, God Created Allotments
The Age to Come
What if money grew on trees (*editor*)

Unheard, Unseen: Submarine E14 and the
Dardanelles
Broke: How to survive the middle class crisis
Alan Turing: Unlocking the Enigma
Peace on Earth: The Christmas truce of 1914
Jerusalem: England's National Anthem
Give and Take (with Sarah Bird)
People Powered Prosperity (with Tony Greenham)
Rupert Brooke: England's Last Patriot
How to be English
Operation Primrose
Before Enigma
The Piper (fiction)
Scandal
How to become a freelance writer

**See also our website at
www.therealpress.couk**